Letters
for the
Culture

To order additional copies of this book, contact:
Xlibris
844-714-8691
www.Xlibris.com
Orders@Xlibris.com

ISBN: 978-1-6698-5416-6 (sc)
ISBN: 978-1-6698-5417-3 (hc)
ISBN: 978-1-6698-5418-0 (e)

Library of Congress Control Number: 2022920421

Print information available on the last page

Rev. date: 06/26/2024

The Letter A is for
Africa

The Letter B is for
Beautiful

Cassava

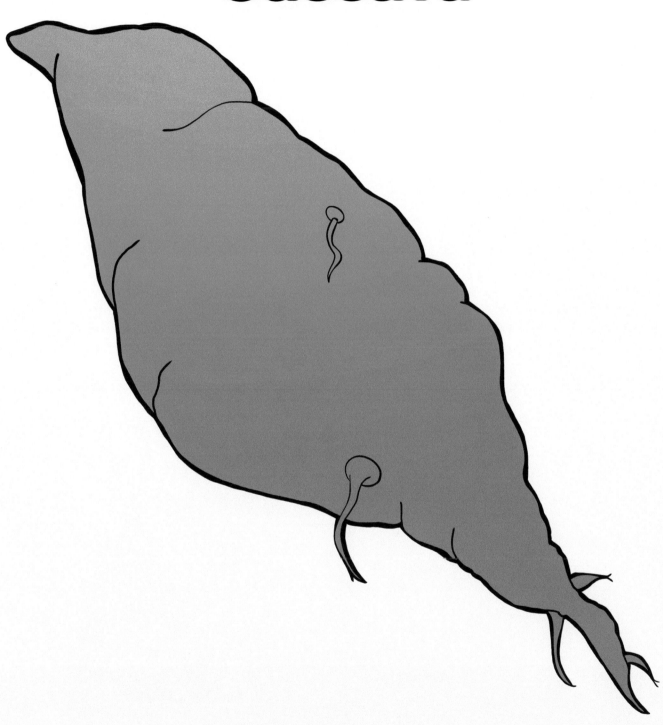

The Letter D is for
Dancing

The Letter E is for
Empress

The Letter F is for
Family

The Letter G is for
Grandma

The Letter H is for
Hip-Hop

The Letter I is for
Island

The Letter J is for
Jackfruit

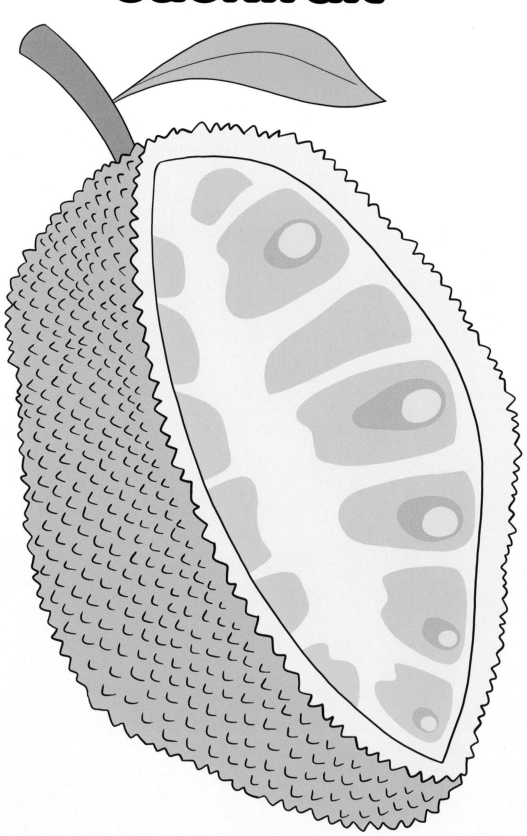

The Letter K is for
Kentay Cloth

The Letter L is for
Love

The Letter M is for
Magic

The Letter N is for
Net

The Letter O is for
Ocean

The Letter P is for
Parade

The Letter Q is for
Quilt

The Letter R is for
Rice

The Letter S is for
Sunset

The Letter T is for
Temple

The Letter U is for
Unity

The Letter V is for
Village

The Letter W is for

Well

The Letter X is for
Xylophone

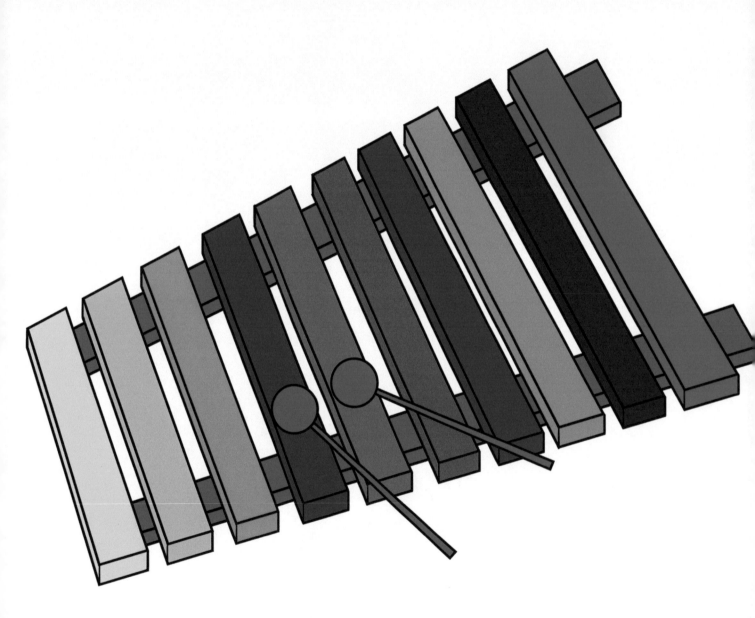

The Letter Y is for
Yam

The Letter Z is for
Zebra